The
KING of
Instruments

The
KING of
Instruments

RICHARD C. GREENE

Carolrhoda Books, Inc., Minneapolis

Many people helped in the preparation of this book. My special thanks to Susan Pearson, Stephen Ryan Oliver, Neal Holtan, Nancy Lancaster, Dr. Richard Waggoner, Dr. John Eggert, Roger Burg, Sr. Elaine Fraher, Kathryn Ullviden Moen, Gary Thomas, Sam Marks, Curt Oliver, Roger Ide, and Craig Bodine.

Cover design by Gale Houdek
Text design by David Barnard

LIBRARY OF CONGRESS CATALOGING IN PUBLICATION DATA

Greene, Richard C.
    The king of instruments.

    Summary: Text and photographs explain the workings of
the world's largest musical instrument, the pipe organ.
    1. Organ—Juvenile literature. 2. Organs—Pictorial
works. [1. Organ] I. Title.
ML3930.A2G76   786.6   82-4282
ISBN 0-87614-186-6   AACR2

1 2 3 4 5 6 7 8 9 10 90 89 88 87 86 85 84 83 82

*to Mom and Dad, Jeanne, John, and Dan – my family;
to John Shawhan – who took the time to teach me
about pipe organs; and, of course, to J-R*

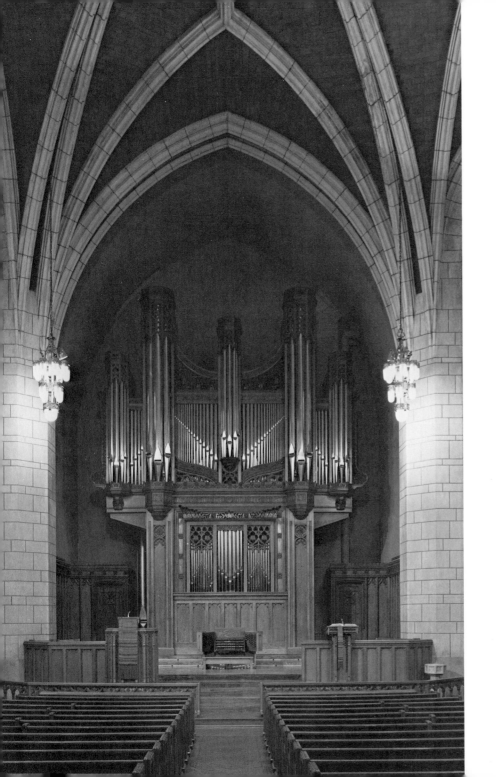

Organs have existed in one form or another for over 2,000 years. They have inspired composers to create masterpieces. For centuries their music has inspired people to worship.

Today there are three common
types of organs.

Some of them make their sounds by
forcing air through reeds. These are
called REED ORGANS. (A reed is a
piece of metal that vibrates when
the wind passes over it. Harmonicas,
sometimes called "mouth organs,"
work in this way too.)

Others make their sounds elec-
tronically. These are called ELEC-
TRONIC ORGANS.

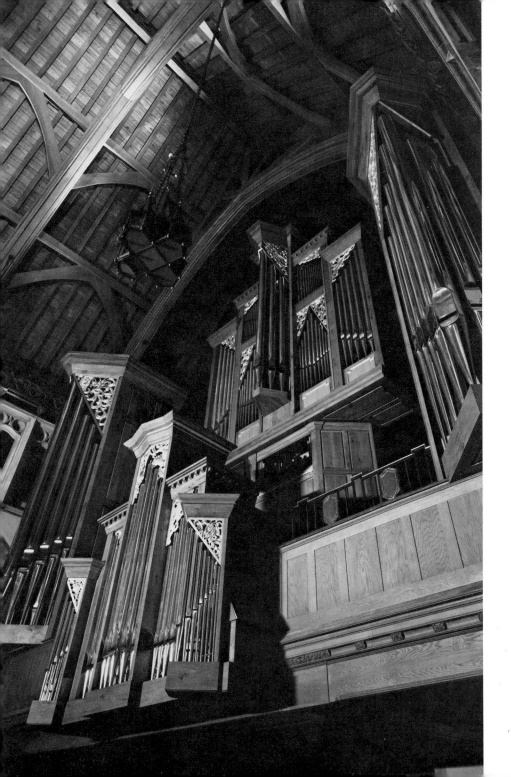

But the most majestic-looking organs – the organs whose shiny pipes glisten and whose size we marvel at – make their sounds by blowing air through metal or wooden pipes. These are called PIPE ORGANS.

The pipe organ is the largest and most powerful of all musical instruments. Although a small pipe organ may have only a few hundred pipes, a large pipe organ could have thousands! A large pipe organ can make soft, delicate music, or it can match the strength of a symphony orchestra. No wonder it's often called the King of Instruments.

Although a large pipe organ looks extremely complicated, it really isn't. In fact, the pipes work very much like a simple whistle works when it's blown.

In every pipe organ the sound begins with a BLOWER. Usually the blower is operated by an electric motor. The blower blows air into a chamber called a WINDCHEST.

The pipes sit on the windchest. At the bottom of each pipe is a valve. The valve keeps the air out of the pipe until the pipe is ready to be played.

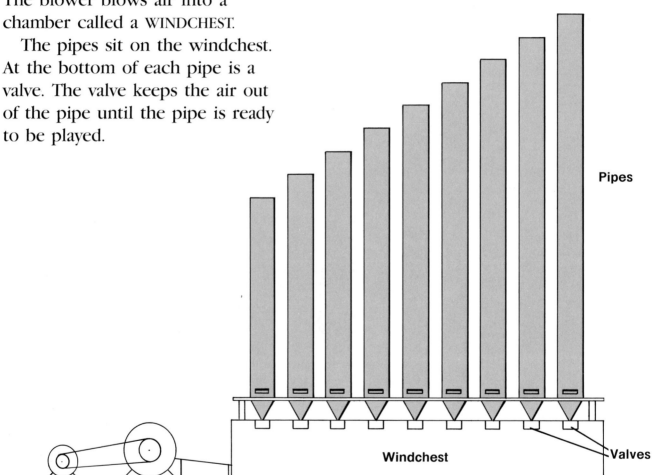

Pipes

Windchest

Valves

Motor   Blower

When the organist presses the key for a particular pipe, the valve opens and lets air from the windchest flow through the pipe. This is what makes the sound.

Pipes come in many different sizes. Some are very large. These will make low, loud sounds. Others are very small. These will make high, bright sounds.

In addition to varying their sizes, pipes can be further designed to make specific sounds.

These pipes have been designed to make soft, smooth sounds.

These will make loud, exciting sounds.

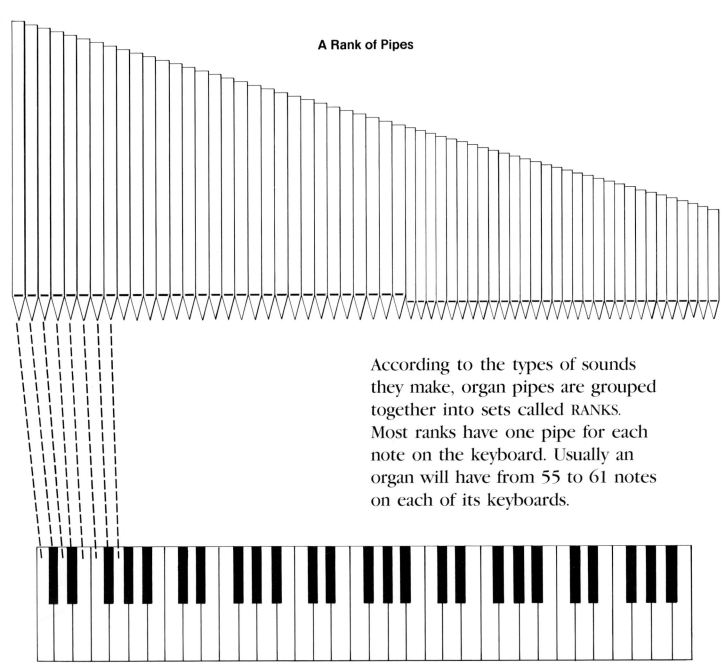

A Rank of Pipes

According to the types of sounds they make, organ pipes are grouped together into sets called RANKS. Most ranks have one pipe for each note on the keyboard. Usually an organ will have from 55 to 61 notes on each of its keyboards.

Keyboard

Organs come in many different sizes. Some have only one keyboard, or MANUAL, and just one rank of pipes.

Others have as many as seven manuals and several hundred ranks! Several manuals allow the organist to play a rank that makes one kind of sound on one manual, and at the same time play ranks that make other kinds of sounds on other manuals.

The organist sits at the controls of
the organ. This area is called the
CONSOLE.

The console is another part of a pipe organ that looks complicated but really isn't. Each manual is just like a piano keyboard.

The knobs on the sides of the console are called STOPS. A stop is a switch for turning ranks on and off. Before playing a piece of music, the organist chooses which ranks to use and turns on those ranks by pulling out the right stop knobs. For example, the organist may need a soft, flutey sound to start with, so he or she would choose a flutey-sounding rank for the top manual. On the second manual some violin-sounding ranks might be chosen to go with the soft flute. Next the piece of music might call for some loud, exciting sounds, so the organist might select a trumpet-sounding rank for the third manual. To end the piece, the organist might choose to play a combination of flute, cello, and violin sounds on the fourth manual. Which ranks are played on which manuals is completely up to the organist.

The small buttons between each manual are called PRE-SETS. They allow the organist to change the ranks being played on that manual in the middle of a piece of music. For example, if the organist only needed those soft, flutey sounds occasionally during the piece, but in between needed a brass choir effect, the organist could choose a second selection of ranks to be played on the top manual. Before beginning to play, the organist would program a pre-set for the brass choir. Then, when the time came to change the ranks played on the first manual, all the organist would have to do is push that pre-set button.

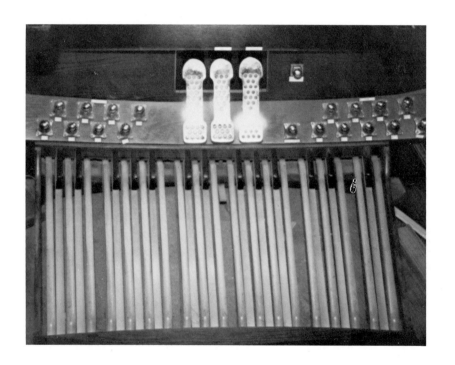

Pipe organs also have foot pedals. Most of these pedals make up a keyboard, like a piano keyboard, that the organist plays with both feet.

The pedals at the top of the picture that are shiny and look like the bottom of a shoe are called SWELL PEDALS. They work like the accelerator in a car and make the music louder or softer.

The knobs to the left and right of the swell pedals are pre-sets, called TOE STUDS, that the organist can set with his or her feet.

There are some pipes in an organ that are more useful if the organist can make them sound louder or softer. These pipes are put into a large enclosure called a SWELL BOX.

The swell box has SHUTTERS on the front that open and close. These shutters are controlled by the swell pedals. When the shutters are open, the pipes are heard clearly.

When the shutters are closed, the
same pipes are heard more softly.

The organist can only vary the
volume of pipes that are in swell
boxes. The pipes that you can see are
pipes that can be played at only
one volume.

Pipe organs are found in many places. They are found in people's homes …

25

...and in auditoriums, and in
many other places. But mainly they
are found in churches, synagogues,
and cathedrals.

Some pipe organ pipes are visible.   Others are hidden.

Some windchests and pipes are on
the walls.

Others are held in wooden cases.

But all of these organs have one
thing in common: Their sounds are
made with pipes. That's why they're
called pipe organs.

Index of Organs

cover   C.B. Fisk organ, House of Hope Presbyterian Church, St.Paul, Minnesota

page 2   Robert Sipe organ, Hennepin Avenue United Methodist Church, Minneapolis, Minnesota
photograph by Warren Reynolds/Warren Reynolds & Associates

page 6   Robert Sipe organ, Hennepin Avenue Methodist Church, Minneapolis
photograph by Warren Reynolds/Warren Reynolds & Associates

page 7   Estey reed organ, Cathedral of St. Paul, St. Paul
Hammond electronic organ, Bodines, Inc., Minneapolis

page 8   C. B. Fisk organ, House of Hope Presbyterian Church, St. Paul
photograph by Bob Olsgard

page 15   Orvold portativ, Church of the Sacred Heart, St. Paul

page 16   C. B. Fisk organ, House of Hope Presbyterian Church, St. Paul
Aeolian-Skinner organ, Macalester College, St. Paul

pages 19, 20, 21   Cassavant organ, Central Lutheran Church, Minneapolis

pages 22, 23, 24   Schlicker organ, Concordia College, St. Paul

page 25   Helmutt Wolff organ, private residence, St. Paul
Geoffrey Hunt organ, private residence, St. Paul

page 26   Aeolian-Skinner organ, Macalester College, St. Paul

page 27   Holtkamp organ, Woodlake Lutheran Church, Richfield, Minnesota (exposed)
Moeller organ, Gustavus Adolphus Lutheran Church, St. Paul (enclosed)

page 28   Shantz organ, Richfield Lutheran Church, Richfield, Minnesota
photograph by Nordin Studio, Minneapolis

page 29   Dobson organ, Olivet Congregational Church, St. Paul

page 30   Schlicker organ, Concordia College, St. Paul

page 31   C. B. Fisk organ, House of Hope Presbyterian Church, St. Paul
photograph by Bob Olsgard

The
KING of
Instruments

RICHARD C. GREENE

Of all the musical instruments in the world, which is the biggest? Which is the most powerful? The answer to both questions is the same: the pipe organ. A large pipe organ may have thousands and thousands of pipes. It can make soft, whispering sounds, or it can boom out with the strength of a complete symphony orchestra! No wonder it's called the King of Instruments.

Although most of us have seen a pipe organ, admired its glistening pipes, and been awed by its music at least once, not many of us have the slightest idea of how it works. Now Richard C. Greene takes readers step by step through a simple explanation of the workings of a pipe organ. His sharp, clear photographs highlight every detail and will leave readers marveling at the amazing King of Instruments.